Shaped
by God's Hand
Pastor Ralph Olsen

Inspiring Voices®

A Service of **Guideposts**

Inspiring Voices books may be ordered through booksellers or by contacting:

Inspiring Voices
1663 Liberty Drive
Bloomington, IN 47403
www.inspiringvoices.com
1-(866) 697-5313

Because of the dynamic nature of the Internet, any web addresses or links contained in this book may have changed since publication and may no longer be valid. The views expressed in this work are solely those of the author and do not necessarily reflect the views of the publisher, and the publisher hereby disclaims any responsibility for them.

Any people depicted in stock imagery provided by Thinkstock are models, and such images are being used for illustrative purposes only.

Certain stock imagery © Thinkstock.

ISBN: 978-1-4624-0491-9 (sc)
ISBN: 978-1-4624-0490-2 (e)

Printed in the United States of America

Inspiring Voices rev. date: 2/1/2013

Dedication

In the fifteenth year of ministry, I found myself asking the question, "Lord, is this how you really want me to spend the rest of my life?" I sought advice from a trusted friend who was an executive for a major corporation in Minnesota. At the end of a long lunch and conversation he said to me, "Ralph, if your goal in life is to make money there are companies always looking for people with your skills and passion. Yet, as I heard you talk about mission and ministry I noticed something; your face lights up like a Christmas tree, your hands become animated and move in multiple directions and your eyes twinkle like stars in the dark, night sky. This tells me you are precisely in the vocation of God's plan for your life. At the end of your ministry your riches may not be accumulated wealth or possessions, rather your riches will be in the relationships you shared with people locally and around the world by your vision, witness, encouragement, love, laughter and enthusiasm for life." He was right!

I dedicate this book with love to my family: my wife, Andrea, my children, Emily, Elise, Erica, Jeffrey and grandson Sam; and to all the members of my large extended family.

I have been inspired by the leadership, wisdom and encouragement of Pastors Richard Swanson, David Pearson, Gary Langness, Dr. Fred Marks, Bishop Herbert Chilstrom and missionaries Dr. Mark and Linda Jacobson. With thanks to the people of Augustana Lutheran Church, King of Kings Lutheran Church and Kilolo Parish, Tanzania, it has been my privilege to serve with you in the Lord's service.

Each of you have inspired me to dream big, be a compassionate witness of Christ's love grounded in the words of the prophet Micah 6:8, "What does the Lord require of you; only this, to act justly, love tenderly and walk humbly with your God."

I am a blessed man!

Grandson Samuel James and Gumpa Ralph

Why write a book?

I write this book for two reasons: to honor Grandpa J. S. Helling, the family historian on my wife's side. Grandpa shared with the family many times the history of the Treaty of Traverse Des Sioux, because from that treaty the Helling family acquired prime farm land in southwestern Minnesota. Grandpa wanted future generations of the family to remember how the family received the land and was blessed with the richness of crops that had been grown through the years. I don't remember how many times we said to each other we should preserve this history by recording Grandpa Helling re-telling the story in his voice, but we didn't. Grandpa died at the age of 99 years. The second reason I write this book as my legacy gift to my children, my grandson Samuel and any grandchildren yet to be born that the spirit of my life will live on through the witness of their lives.

Grandparents J.S. and Stella Helling

My story begins two years before my birth. On July 17th, 1947, Ralph Harold Olsen married Kaye Marion Paulick, my parents. My father was a smart man who found school not very challenging so he dropped out after ninth grade. He spent his working years as a machinist in various factories. My mother worked part time as a secretary. They lived a simple life in a small apartment on Chicago's north side and spent their weekends bowling and playing cards with their friends. Cribbage was their favorite card game and it would become mine, too, in the coming years.

Ralph and Kaye Olsen, my parents, on
their wedding day, July 17, 1947

It wasn't long before life as they knew it would change. On May 18, 1949 I made my entry into the world at Illinois Masonic Hospital in Chicago, Illinois. When the doctor announced I was healthy baby boy my mother was shocked as she was expecting a baby girl. You see, in those days the use of ultrasound didn't exist, so doctors made educated guesses as to the sex of a baby by listening to the heart beat. It was thought that a rapid heartbeat was probably a girl and a slow heartbeat a boy. My mother remembers that my heart beat as fast as a race horse runs so based on the doctor's guess they chose only a girl's name for their child – Christine Marie Olsen. As first time parents they hadn't considered the possibility that their soon to be born child might be a boy. Needless to say they were surprised!

So, for the first couple days of my life I was known as "Baby Boy Olsen." When the time came to bring me home the nurse told my father I could not be released without a name on the birth certificate. Without consulting my mother my dad proudly announced to the nurse, "His name is Ralph Harold Olsen, Jr.," and that's how I got my name.

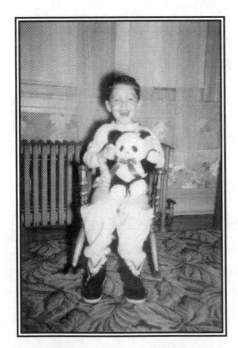

Christmas in our garden apartment with my only present, Seymour the Bear

My first home was a garden apartment on Ravenswood Avenue in Chicago. Garden apartments may sound neat, but actually it was an apartment in the lower level of a building with windows at ground level. As a young boy I would stand on the sofa and look at all the feet passing by each day wondering where they were going. When I asked my mother where they were going she only said, "Someday you will know." My mother had some interesting ways of answering questions. Growing up in the city was a unique experience. The city offered so much, but lacked one thing – parks and playgrounds. The buildings were very close together, usually separated only by a sidewalk. My grandparents lived in an apartment on the third floor and when I was at their place I would call out through the window to Johnny, a boy my age, and ask what his family was having for dinner and if he wanted to trade because the buildings were so close to each other I thought we could pass the meals from window to window!

The nearest playground was about eight blocks away at my elementary school which meant my friends and I would usually play ball in the alley behind the apartment. The alley was, also, the place where my father tried to teach me how to ride a bike. He would put me on the seat, give me a strong push and yell, "Junior, keep the handlebar straight and keep peddling." Honestly, I wasn't very good at pedaling and steering at the same time so it was inevitable that I would crash into a garage or garbage can. After several attempts I was often bleeding, bruised and crying, so I would give up and go back to the apartment. My dad would shout, "Son, you're hopeless. If you keep quitting you'll never learn to ride a bike and that means you'll just have to walk your bike everywhere!"

My life was rolling along pretty good until January 19, 1954 when my sister, Alison Kaye, was born. Who was this crying creature all through the night? Will I never get another night of sleep? Why do I have to share? Why do I have to watch her instead of playing with my friends? Of course, I was the recipient of many lectures about being a good big brother and wasn't it a blessing to have a sister. I didn't agree. The five year age difference between us was enough that we were like two only children. We went our own ways and tried to ignore each other. Unfortunately, over the years our relationship with each other never changed. Alison saw me as the silver spoon brother who received everything he ever wanted while she got the leftovers. I thought she was lazy and believed she could achieve anything she desired. When our father died in 2011, I didn't know where she lived or even how to contact her. That fact haunts me to this day and I hope someday, God willing, he will lead us to reconcile.

In 1959 my parents built their first home in Mundelein, Illinois, thirty miles north of Chicago. They paid a whopping $16,000 for the house at 105 S. Lake Street! Best of all, I would have my own bedroom! It didn't even matter to me that it was the smallest bedroom. The room was so small it could only fit a bed and a desk which left about 12" of space to walk. Still the first time I saw the house I thought it was a castle. Windows weren't on the ground. There was a backyard to play in. The neighbor houses were more than three feet away. This surely was a blessing to our family.

I made friends quickly and remember the many summer adventures we shared. However, I had a problem. I still couldn't ride a bike. My father, true to his word, said since I couldn't ride my bike I would have to walk it everywhere I went. Being left behind while your friends ride off to new discoveries didn't take me long to realize I needed to learn how to ride a bike, and do it fast. One Sunday afternoon, my cousin, Dara Paulick was visiting and she took me to the nearby school to teach me how to ride my bike. She said we weren't coming home until I could do it! I thought to myself this is going to be a long night. It was a shaky start with several crashes. Dara didn't yell, was very encouraging and after forty-five minutes I rode home triumphantly to share the good news. My father said two words, "About time."

I liked elementary school, the teachers and baseball card drop during recess. The game consisted of placing a card you didn't want or had more than one of it on the ground up to 12" from the wall. Each person would take another card, hold it against the wall at about a height of 3', and let it drop. If your card fell on a card and covered at least half of the card it was yours. As I look back on baseball card drop it was pretty fundamental but kept us boys busy during many a recess.

I do remember having a crush on Rhonda Wilson in fifth grade. Every day during recess I would watch Rhonda play jacks with her friends. She was the cutest girl I knew and I was convinced she didn't really know I existed. I thought if I learned to play jacks maybe she would want to be my girl friend. I bought jacks and practiced every day until I thought I was ready. Boldly, I walked up to Rhonda and asked if I could play. She said she didn't mind. I started out like a ball of fire feeling quite confident that after I won the game Rhonda would be my girl friend. Needless to say, she quickly deflated that idea! I walked away unlucky in jacks and unlucky in love.

I was active in Cub Scout Pack 77 with my friends. My least favorite activity as a scout was the boring Memorial Day parade we marched in every year. Why was it always hot? Why were the speeches so boring?

My Cub Scout den after a long parade march
for Memorial Day, May 31, 1959

I entered a car every year in the Soapbox Derby. I never even came close to winning or placing for a ribbon. I never had help from my father like the other boys. Their cars were built for speed and looked it, while my car looked like I made it with junk from the scrap yard.

An unforgettable moment of Cub Scouts and maybe the beginning of my acting career was the play, "Mother has Bubble Troubles." I was chosen by my friends to be the Mother which meant I had to wear a white mop for hair and a flowered apron. My mother said I was so cute, and maybe was meant to be a girl, which, of course, my friends had many good laughs over that. I thought it takes guts to play the role of mother before the entire pack and their parents.

Mother Has Bubble Troubles

In seventh grade I began to realize my family was different from other families. When I would go to a friend's house everyone seemed happy. No yelling or screaming like I knew at home. Other dads and moms went to work and came home for a nice family dinner. My father would frequently stop at the local tavern, the Chug-A-Lug for a couple of bumps (drinks), before coming home. As the tavern was a block from our house my mother would send me to bring my father home when it was time for dinner. Dinners were often filled with arguing and yelling. Times were difficult for our family as there always seemed to be a crisis. Our power was turned off more than once because we could not pay our bill. One Christmas we had no money for a Christmas tree or even a present because my father had spent his check on booze and shooting pool. A miracle happened that Christmas Eve night as a mysterious visitor left a tree and some presents at our front door. Squeals of joy came from our house when we discovered those gifts on Christmas morning. Several years later I learned our neighbor, George, had been Secret Santa. This had to be a H.S.M. (Holy Spirit Moment) because George and my father never got along. They were always arguing and swearing at each other about something. I think they really liked each other and did those things just for show.

As I look back I didn't realize it at the time or even understand the word surrogate, but through everything I had experienced I had become a surrogate husband for my mother at the age of ten. I was the man of the house the emotional strength and support for my mother. Meanwhile my father and I drifted apart. I became very involved in school activities such as basketball, choir, pep club, student government and several other clubs. School was my safe haven from the problems at home and in my senior year my classmates named me the person with the Most School Spirit.

It was this period of my life that I began my faith journey. My mother was a positive and moral influence on my life though she didn't go to church. She lived her life by example teaching me to be kind to all people, respect people of all colors and races and see life as an exciting adventure. Mom wanted more than anything for our family to join a church and worship together in hopes that my father would come back to the church. Unfortunately, that never happened in her life. My father was raised Lutheran through my Grandmother, Teresa, always said she was Catholic. When my father was sixteen his younger sister died from leukemia, he prayed every day that God would heal her. When she died he left the church and never returned until my mother died in 1993 and he attended her funeral. His reason was "If God were truly a God of love and grace he would have healed his sister. In the years to come there would be many conversations about my father's faith or lack of it. Little did anyone know at the time the vocational path I would take later in my life.

This seems like a good place to interject the beginning of my faith journey. My mother was a very positive and moral influence in my life though she didn't go to church. She taught me values by her example of kindness to others, teaching me that all people are uniquely created by God and there is so much we can learn so much by taking time to get to know others. She demonstrated by example what service means and that we should always strive to see the positive in life because it is so easy to see the negative in life. Mom wanted more than anything for our family to join a church and worship together in hopes that my father would come back to the church. Unfortunately, this never happened during her life. My father was raised in the Lutheran faith even though my Grandmother Theresa always said she was Catholic. Dad went to confirmation and youth group in his teens, but when his younger sister died from leukemia he gave up on God and the church. He said he prayed to God every day that his sister be healed and not die. That was not to be the case. He left the church and never returned. His reason, "If God is truly a God of love and grace he would have saved my sister." In the years ahead there would be many conversations about my father's faith or lack of it. Little did anyone know the vocational path I would take later in life.

When I was in fifth grade I watched my friends walk by our house about the same time every Sunday morning. Puzzled by this, one Sunday I went outside and asked them where they were going. They said Sunday school and asked me if I want to come along. I went inside to ask my mother and she wanted to know what faith they were so I went outside to find out. When I asked them what faith they were, at first, they looked like deer caught in headlights of a car. They said they were going to St. Andrew's Lutheran Church and when I told my mother she said I could go. When I came home later that morning I asked my mother why she wanted to know what faith they were. There were two churches two blocks from our home St. Andrew's Lutheran and across the street Santa Maria Del Popolo. My mother told me she didn't want me to go to the Catholic Church and when I asked her why she said something about they do not eat meant on Fridays or something like that. It was an odd response, but one I accepted.

In seventh grade I started Confirmation classes with my friends. There's a saying, "If the kids become involved parents usually follow." In my case it was my mother who joined St. Andrews and became very involved teaching Sunday school and helping in many of the women's areas. Confirmation class was three years, every Saturday morning during the school year for two hours! At the end of the three years there was the public night open to the congregation where we had the opportunity to share what we had learned, commonly known by we, confimands, as the Grand Inquisition. On a Thursday night two weeks before Confirmation Sunday we sat in the front pews of the sanctuary which was packed with parents and church members. Our pastor, Harold Wimmer, stood in the pulpit and called one name at a time to stand and answer one question from three years of studying and memorizing Luther's Catechism. I must have been in a daze when my name was called, because a classmate poked me and said it's your turn. Pastor Wimmer using our full name said, "Ralph Harold Olsen Jr." please stand. I rose and thought my heart had left my body. "Can you name the creeds of the church?" I quickly said, "Apostles, Nicene and Athanasian," and sat down relieved. "Ralph Harold Olsen Jr. please rise," came pastor's voice. What? I answered my question. "Son, you're not finished. Please recite the creeds of the church," He must be kidding! I don't think any of us can do that. Nevertheless, I recited the Apostle and Nicene Creeds perfectly. As I began the Athanasian Creed I managed to recite three paragraphs and then froze. Trembling, I said, "That's all I know," and sat down convinced I had just flunked confirmation. "Ralph Harold Olsen Jr. please rise." Now what, I thought, so I stood up again. "Well done, son, you did better than I expected,' said Pastor Wimmer. 'Now you're finished." I was confirmed on Pentecost Sunday, June 3rd, 1963.

My Confirmation photo, 1963 with Linda
Santee, Pastor Harold Wimmer and me

In the summer between ninth grade and high school I participated in track. I will admit I was not born to run like a lion, I waddled more like a duck. It was also the summer I learned in a personal way something about racial discrimination and prejudice. Through track I met Arthur, an African-American teen, who went to another area school. He was gifted with the ability to run like a cheetah. I had the "lucky" opportunity to run against him in the 440 race twice that summer. All I vividly remember was the cloud of dust I ran through as Arthur passed me to win both races. We became friends and after one meet I invited him to my house for something to eat and hang out for awhile. My father was sitting at the kitchen table drinking a beer when we arrived. He looked at the two of us, spoke a curt hello to Arthur and left the house for the tavern. Embarrassed, my mother quickly invited us to sit down at the table while she brought out a variety of snacks and pop. Arthur stayed about an hour and then his mother picked him up.

When my father returned from the tavern later that afternoon he began berating my friend. The names and words he used that day cannot be repeated in this book. His message was very clear. Arthur was not welcome in our home. While living in the inner city of Chicago I had heard many negative adjectives used to describe people of color and race. Until that day I never realized how hurtful and derogatory those expressions were to people of color and race. My life experiences as the father of three daughters has taught me that small children do not distinguish between race, color or creed. They accept all people just as they are. As they grow older they come to know about prejudice by example and experience from others. I realized later that the words of Dr. Martin Luther King, Jr. spoken at the Lincoln Memorial in Washington, D.C. on August 28, 1963, "I have a dream that one day my children will not be judged by the color of their skin, but by the content of their character," is a mandate for the future of our nation and world. I have committed my life to building bridges of hope and understanding between people, not the opposite. It is imperative that we teach our children that love and understanding, not hatred and war, are the keys to creating a better world for all. How will our children learn if we parents, teachers and other adults do not "walk the talk" living by positive example.

That same summer, I went to work with my father in the factory. I was assigned to the drill press line. Eight hours a day I drilled one hole in a small piece of metal. At the end of every day I came home smelling like grease and oil with hands cut by little slivers of metal. After two weeks I received my first paycheck. I was a rich man with $53.00 in my pocket. At dinner that evening my father said, "How much did you make?" "$53.00," I said. "You owe your mother and me $12 for your room and board. It's important that you understand there is no such thing as a free ride," said my father. I didn't think this was quite fair, but this life lesson taught me the need to be responsible. It didn't take me long to realize I wanted a better life than working in a factory. One night at the dinner table I announced I wanted to go to college. My father told me I was a dreamer because no one in our family had ever gone to college. There was no money so I would have to work in the factory and like it. I thought to myself I will just find a way to earn the money needed. That night my mother came into my room before I went to bed, and as we talked she said she believed in me and with God's help she believed I would receive opportunities for jobs to accomplish my goals. On the day I graduated from college it was a day of celebration none of us ever forgot.

As I prepared to enter high school in the fall of 1963, I wondered how the transition would be as the two junior highs in town were going to be together in the high school. Diamond Lake Jr. High was located on the south side of town and Carl Sandburg on the north side. Each school had a stereotypical image. Kids who went to Carl Sandburg were perceived as "uppity snobs." Kids from Diamond Lake were portrayed as coming from the "wrong side of the tracks."

There was a deep rivalry between the schools, especially when we played each other in basketball. The games were more like a war than basketball. As I recall more often than not we split the two games each year. Community dances were held on Friday nights that summer, which were interesting because the kids from each school stayed on opposite sides of the gym looking at each other. If anyone danced it was mostly the girls while the guys stood against the wall trying to look cool. I had met a girl from Diamond Lake in track. Karen was like my friend, Arthur, in track. She could run fast and I thought she was very cute.

One Friday night as I was standing against the wall in the gym as we always did, I told my friends I was going to ask Karen to dance. Startled they said I was asking for trouble. Not to be deterred I walked to the other side of the gym and asked her if she would like to dance. She said yes and when the song came to an end I thanked her, we parted and went back to our respective sides.

Later that night as I was using the restroom several guys from Diamond Lake came in and told me in no uncertain terms to stay away from their women or I would be sorry. Since that made no sense to me I crossed the line again to ask Karen to dance. I could see by the look in their eyes I had gone too far. When the dance was over I quickly left the building and ran to the car where my mom was waiting to take me home.

The next week while riding my bike I was stopped by the guys from the restroom at the dance. Two guys pulled me off my bike and one said to me, "Didn't we tell you to leave our women alone or there would be consequences." The next thing I remember was a fist coming at me and landing right between my eyes knocking me to the ground. "Get up and fight like a man," one of them said to me. Even though my father always told me there might come a time when I would need to defend myself, I didn't believe retaliating was the way to resolve situations. Fighting made you no better than those who started the fight. They taunted me to get up and fight like a man and I told them they could do what they wanted, but there was no way I would get up. "You are nothing more than a big chicken," they said as they walked away laughing and clucking like a brood of chickens.

End of story – not really, for on the first day of high school I was at my locker which had been assigned alphabetically by grade. Suddenly, there was a hand on my shoulder, I turned and saw the boy who had slugged me. His locker was next to mine and with him were four other friends. Smiling he said to me, "Olsen, we decided you're not a chicken. You've got guts. So, we decided you can dance with any of our women whenever you want." "Thank you," I said, though I knew I could dance with any girl any time. The lesson I learned from this experience was to take the high road remain true to your principles. In the eighth chapter of the book of John, Jesus said, "If you continue in my word, you are truly my disciples, and you will know the truth and the truth will set you free." To be a person of integrity is the most important characteristic one can have in their life.

In the fall of my junior year in high school I told my guidance counselor, Mr. Nelson, and my choir director, Ms. Mitchell, I was planning to go to college. Both said that was a worthy goal and each gave me some practical advice. "Your grades are decent, but I don't believe high enough for admission to a private college. I would look at state colleges where you would have a better chance for admission,' said Mr. Nelson. Ms. Mitchell said, "You have a good voice. I hope you will continue to sing in college, but don't be disappointed if you don't make the top choir. It is very select." This was the first time I remember any of my teachers telling me I wasn't good enough to do something. I was surprised but this only affirmed my resolve to do it.

The final two years of high school flew by. I was active in student government, choir, pep club, state solo, octet and quartet competitions and several other organizations. The highlight of senior year came when I was chosen to play the male lead in the spring musical, "Plain and Fancy." It was the story of two young Amish adults who are in love, but her father has prearranged for his daughter to marry a much older man she doesn't love. Cindy Dahm was chosen to be the female lead. I knew this might be trouble because Cindy lived a block away from my house and we had known each other since elementary school. I spent so much time at her house shooting hoops with her father, who said I was like a brother to Cindy. Secretly, I had a huge crush on her, but never said anything. Rehearsals were going well until we came to the point in the play where I was to profess my love and kiss her. Every time we got close enough to do the kissing scene we burst out laughing. We couldn't do it. The drama teacher tried every trick in the book to help us, to no avail. After re-doing the scene too many times to count the director said, "If the two of you can't do the scene right by tomorrow I will replace you!" That night at Cindy's house we rehearsed and rehearsed to no avail until her sister, Patty, found a way for us to get close enough so it looked like we were kissing, but in reality we weren't. The play, itself, was not one of the more popular plays of the time. Still we had good attendance at every performance. On the last night after the final bow and closing of the curtain Cindy and I gave each other a big hug and said, "We did it." The hug was nice, but I really wanted to kiss her.

Following graduation, I worked several jobs that summer to raise money for college. Contrary to what some believed, I was accepted for admission to Augustana College, Rock Island, Illinois, a private college affiliated with the Lutheran Church in America. Even more surprising, I made the Augustana Choir, the top choir, as a freshman and had the privilege to sing in the choir all four years. I don't know if it was just luck or maybe part of God's plan for me to be in choir. Being a tenor I was fortunate because that fall they needed 5 tenors to fill the eight spots in that section. Ten years after graduating the choir came to Minnesota as part of their spring tour. At an alumni dinner I sat at the table with the director, Don Morrison. Our table was reminiscing about the good old days when Mr. Morrison said, "Olsen, you know I didn't pick you for choir because of your voice. I could see that you would be an energizer for the choir with your personality and positive attitude. You were never sick on tour. You never let me down. You were the champion cheerleader and kept everyone looking up, even after the upper classmen pranked you numerous times with the old Ultra Brite toothpaste in your mouth while you were sleeping trick!" Looking back over that experience I don't think my being in the choir was luck, rather it was a small part of God's plan for my life.

College was very different from high school. No mom to wake me in the morning. I was responsible for everything, even washing my clothes. Like most new college students my first two attempts at laundry featured some very interesting color combinations. Unlike high school, I didn't have class every hour all day. I had no class on Tuesday or Thursday except for choir at 4 p.m.

I liked the freedom of college, maybe a bit too much. Besides singing in choir I pledged Omicron Sigma Omicron fraternity and went to many social events and activities. Free time in the dorm lounge most often found me playing cribbage and euchre with my friends. At the end of my freshman year I received a letter from the Dean of Students informing me my grade point was a whopping 1.87! I needed a 2.0 or better if I wanted to stay in school. The dean placed me on academic probation" which meant I had one semester to raise my grade point average to 2.0 or better, or I was out. Out! Kicked out of college! My dream shattered. No way was I going back to work in the factory. I needed to get my act together.

Grandma Daisy Martine, me and my mom on graduation day at Augustana College

Something had to change and it would that fall in a speech class with Dr. Theodore LeVander and several one – on – one conversations with the campus pastor, Rev. Richard "Swannie" Swanson. Dr. LeVander was a strict taskmaster who expected your best effort every day. Most students dreaded Dr. LeVander's class, but I was drawn to him for some unknown reason that my friends could not understand.

He knew my academic situation and my dream to be the first college graduate in my family.

One day after class he stopped me in the hall and said, "Olsen, if you're willing to work hard, I am willing to be your mentor. As your mentor you will come to my office once a week for the rest of your time here at Augustana. I will review your progress. I will mentor you as long as you are willing to work. Is it a deal?" "Yes," I answered. Over the course of the next three years we met weekly. I am indebted to Dr. LeVander for my proficiency as a public speaker today. One the day of graduation after the ceremony Dr. LeVander sought me on the stadium field and told me I had come a long way since we first met. I had earned a degree that others had said would be impossible for me. He said it had been a pleasure to be my instructor and mentor and he believed that no matter what path I chose in the future I would be very successful.

"Swannie" was a man of quiet demeanor, full of compassion and understanding. He had a wonderful way with words. He could encourage you to see the positive even in tough times, while at the same time provide direct and firm guidance when needed without making you feel like a failure. Both men are with their Savior, Jesus Christ. I look forward to a great reunion with them in eternal life.

In May of 1971, I became the first college graduate in my family with a B.A. degree in Communications and English. It was a proud moment. What I remember from that day were the words of my father, "You did it, Sunny Boy. I'm proud of you." I think that might have been the first time I remember my father saying he was proud of me.

Now, what was next? Where the road would lead I wasn't sure. Still I was sensing God had a plan for my life. That summer I worked part time at my home church. I liked working at the church and enjoyed the conversations I had with Pastor Wimmer. Inevitably, he would guide the conversation toward my going to seminary. I'm not sure what Pastor Wimmer saw in me, but by August I was ready to give it a try because I liked school. When I told my parents I was planning to enter the seminary they were quite surprised. My father said, "You just finished four years of college and you want to go to school for another four years! How will you pay back your loans? You need a job, not more schooling. You don't even know if this is what you want to do with your life." My mother was concerned about my school debt, but said if this was what I wanted to do I could live at home and commute to the seminary in Chicago. No way was I going to do that! I applied to Northwestern Lutheran Seminary, St. Paul, Minnesota. I was accepted for admission and two weeks later I left Chicago to attend a school I had never seen, in a city I had never been to. Was this really part of God's plan for my life? I was going to find out.

Young and naïve I left Chicago about 4:00 p.m. and arrived in St. Paul at 11:00 p.m., but now where do I go? I pulled into a gas station at Interstate 94 and Lexington Ave. to ask for directions. As I got out of the car three large African-American men looked at me with eyes that seemed to say *wrong neighborhood bro.* I said "Can you help me? I'm new to the area and I am looking for Northwestern Lutheran Seminary." "You gonna be a preacher-man?" one asked me. "I'm not sure if that's what the Lord wants for my life, but I'm here to find out." They gave me directions and wished me well. I thought seminary was like college where the student center was open 24 hours a day, I soon found out that was wrong! The building was locked up tighter than a drum. Not knowing where I was exactly in St. Paul I slept in my car.

The next morning I awoke to the sounds of birds chirping. I grabbed my travel kit, went into the building's restroom, shaved, combed my hair and went to the office of admissions. I was assigned to be an advisee of Dr. Walter Buschman. Walt was a down-to-earth guy and loved to laugh. In class I didn't understand much of what the teachers taught. I couldn't quite comprehend how what they were saying could be applied to people in their faith journeys. My saving grace was the new friends I met, three in particular, Paul Hammarberg, Dave Swenson and Bill Bohline. With their help and other classmates I managed to get through the first year and my grades were decent. However, I still wasn't sure if this was God's plan for my life. On the last day of class I walked into Dr. Buschman's office to tell him I wasn't coming back in the fall. "Ok, Olsen, see you in the fall," he said. Wait a minute, didn't he hear what I said so I repeated my plan. "Olsen, do you want to wager on that? If you're back in the fall you owe my wife and I dinner at Mr. Steak in Roseville. Do we have a deal?" Why not, I thought to myself, I know I won't be here in the fall. I said, "Deal," and walked out of his office. Little did I know my life was about to change. God was up to something though I didn't know it.

While eating lunch a man came up and introduced himself, Rev. David Pearson, Senior Pastor of First Lutheran Church, Brainerd, Minnesota. He asked me if I had plans for the summer. I told him I was going back to Chicago because seminary was not for me. Do you have a job for the summer? No, I said. I need someone for the summer to work with youth and help with home-bound visitation. We will provide a place to live, furnished, utilities paid and a monthly stipend for salary and gas for your car. Are you interested? Having nothing to do I said yes, and by mid-afternoon I was on my way to Brainerd.

Seminary Graduation–Jim Nelson, Dave Swenson, Paul Hammerberg, me, Frank Maxwell and Gary Cumings

I enjoyed my summer in Brainerd, especially evening conversations with Pastor David and his wife, Judy, on their front porch. Visiting home-bound members was a wonderful experience as I learned much about their faith and life. I was the recipient of many delicious treats during my visits and because I was single, several folks thought their granddaughters would be perfect as my wife. Sadly, those thoughts never came to fruition. Two months went quickly and I was still unsure if God's plan for my life included ministry.

Ordination at Christ Chapel-Rev. David Pearson, me, Dr. Robert Marshall, Dr. Melvin Hammarberg (page 2 in anniversary book)

One afternoon I stopped at a park to offer a prayer for God to give me a clear answer. "Lord, I'm confused. Maybe it's time for a burning bush or a voice from the clouds to show me your plan. I'm not sure how long I sat there. I remember a breeze gently pass over me. I heard a soft whisper of a voice say, "Ralph, I have called you by name and blessed you with all the gifts you need to serve my people. Trust me and I will lead you in the way."

I returned to seminary that fall, questioning, but trusting God. The first person I saw on campus was Dr. Buschman. All he said was, "Sunday night, 6 p.m. Mr. Steak in Roseville. Don't forget your wallet." During dinner and conversation that evening I asked him how he knew I would return to seminary. "I saw it in your eyes,' he said, 'It was only a matter of time before your head and heart made the connection. Let me tell you something else you will discover along the way. At the end of your ministry your wealth will not be so much in possessions, rather your wealth will be found in the myriad of relationships you will have formed with people all over the world. Your enthusiasm and passion for life will draw people to you and in those relationships you will be blessed. I didn't know it then, but he would be right. Sadly, he died the next year from cancer. In May of 1975 I graduated from seminary. Now, I was the first college and graduate school member of my family.

I was ordained at Christ Chapel on the campus of Gustavus Adolphus College, St. Peter, MN on June 8, 1975, Dr. Robert Marshall, president of the Lutheran Church in America was the presiding officiant at the service of ordination. This was a special moment for me because he had been the president of the Illinois Synod, my home synod, before becoming the president of our national church.

Pastor Gary Langness and I greet guests in Scandinavian dress at Elva Kaffe Festival, Augustana Church

I received a letter of call to serve as Associate Pastor of Augustana

Lutheran Church, West St. Paul, Minnesota, starting that July. Rev. Gary Langness was the Senior Pastor and little did I realize how much I would learn from him in the next five years. The people and young adults of the congregation were amazing. They were excited to try new ministries, help in any way, and took time to say thank you when we succeeded and encouraged me when those new new ideas didn't go as expected. Pastor Gary was a tremendous teacher, excellent preacher and mentor because he "walked the talk." I watched him live what he preached and lead by example every day.

Over the Christmas holiday of 1976, two single women moved in across the hall from my apartment. This had to be God's hand to be so fortunate. They were attractive, fun and we enjoyed doing things together. I tried teaching them racquetball and golf, but I wasn't a very good teacher. A few months after meeting Kathy and Andi, Kathy told me she could see I had taken a shine to Andi, which was true, but I thought she was to beautiful to go out with me. Kathy assured me if I asked she would go. Our first date was June 17, 1977. We went to dinner and a play at the Guthrie Theater in Minneapolis. All I remember of that night was how lucky I felt to be with such a beautiful person. Andi was beautiful in every sense of the word. She was compassionate, kind, deeply devoted to her family, grounded in her faith. She had grown up in rural Minnesota and I in the "windy city" of Chicago. Despite our different backgrounds we shared a common faith and value system. I liked her family right from the start. They enjoyed being together, supported each other, cared for each other and laughed with each other. Good times were plentiful. I felt right at home. Her family was so different than mine. I often teased that she grew up in the Waltons and I was from the Bunkers of television fame!

On August 21st, two months after our first date we got engaged. I hadn't planned for it to happen that day, it just did. In what might be one of the least romantic proposals known to man I said to her,

"Have you ever thought about being a pastor's wife? Yes. Have you ever thought about being this pastor's wife? Yes. Will you marry me? Yes!" That was it. We decided to go ring shopping the next day. On June 17th, 1978 we were married at Zion Lutheran Church, Hanska, Minnesota, exactly one year from our first date.

Andrea did most of the planning for our wedding. I only had two requests for our wedding – 1) I wanted us to memorize our vows and 2) I wanted to choose the music. Andrea had wanted "The Wedding Song" for her wedding, but I said, no. Instead, I chose a classical piece of music that no one in Hanska had ever heard. It was so unknown they probably still talk about it in town. Denise Johnson, a youth group member from Augustana, played flute. It was her first wedding to play for and even though she said she was nervous she did a great job.

Andrea and I on our wedding day

By the time of our wedding Andrea had gotten to know my seminary friends and these guys were a fun, loving bunch. Andrea's admonishment to me for our wedding was that they were to be on their best behavior since everyone in town knew her family. The night of rehearsal started late because Paul and Dave somehow missed the sign for Hanska and found themselves in the next town, Madelia. When they finally got to the church the rehearsal went as planned.

It rained the morning of our wedding. Many people say rain on your wedding day is a sign of good luck. I have heard it said that it is harder to untie a wet knot than a dry knot. We shot the pictures before the wedding and there was some time before the service. Once again, Andrea reminded me to keep an eye on my friends. It didn't take long for me to discover they were missing in action. I thought I better go find them. As I started toward town they were coming across the church lawn. "Where were you?" I asked. They were hungry and had gone to town for something to eat, which just happened to be at the Municipal Liquor store. Over beers and burgers my friends made quite a few new friends in Hanska that day.

It came time for the service. I was standing up front waiting for the doors in the back to open when I saw people smiling and looking at something behind me. I began to wonder what my friends might have done. As I turned around I saw they had removed the hymn numbers from the board and replaced them with "Ralph loves Andi!" I did think that was pretty good and as I turned around I saw Andi and her father, Clayton, ready to come down the aisle.

Andi was radiant. I said a quick prayer to God, "Thank you, God, I am a very lucky man!" We had a traditional Lutheran wedding about 25 minutes long. Following the service we greeted people in the entry as they made their way to the fellowship hall in the basement where my mother-in-laws' circle served ham buns, salads, cake, coffee and punch. The last person to come through the receiving line was Pastor Florence. As he shook my hand he said, "Congratulations, Ralph. There's something I think you should know. Before God, your guests and the numerous pastors you invited to the wedding, during the vows you said you would forgive Andi, but she never said she would forgive you." Now this was the age before video cameras so a small tape player had been set up to record the service. Sure enough he was right! Still, I know for a fact she has forgiven me many times in our marriage.

Unlike modern weddings, our wedding didn't cost $20,000, nor did we have an open bar and dance at the reception. Our wedding started at 2:00 p.m. and everything was over by 4:15 p.m.! Our honeymoon was simple a short trip up Minnesota's north shore and back. One memory from our honeymoon was classic. The first night we stopped in Hinckley, Minnesota to spend the night at Cassidy's Motor Lodge. Located along Interstate 35, Andi asked me to get a room with a view that did not look at the interstate. The desk clerk said, "I have a great room for you." I went to get our luggage and Andi went to the room. When I got to the room she was laughing. "Open the curtains and see the view," she said. I opened the curtains and the room certainly had a view. The only problem was the pine trees were smack-dab right up to the windows. I couldn't see the forest through the trees!

As honeymoons go I would say it wasn't the classiest, nor the most expensive, but it was an adventure we shared and continue to share thirty-four years later as I write this memoir.

One of the highlights of those early years of marriage was our weekly date night at the Cub Foods grocery. Andi's sister, Kerry, and her fiancé, Bill, would tease us about our BIG Friday night out. Ironically, what goes round comes around. Several years later after Kerry and Bill were married who did we see at the Cub Foods on Friday night!

In the summer of 1980 I accepted an appointment to mission development in Woodbury, Minnesota. It was hard to leave a congregation and people we had grown to love. Our time there was filled with so many wonderful memories and experiences. The congregation at Augustana gave us a wonderful appreciation celebration. I smiled, laughed and cried all throughout the program. When it was over Pastor Langness gave me a piece of his down to earth, practical wisdom. "Ralph, if you ever leave another congregation and they have a special event for you as we did today, if you are going to smile, smile; if you are going to cry, cry; don't do both because it makes you look dumb!" I have never forgotten that and little did I know that wisdom would be needed down the road.

Our journey to Woodbury began on Radio Drive in February of 1980. I was standing on the side of the road with Pastor Ron Peterson and Dr. Fred Marks, who would become my supervisors. Dr. Marks said, "Ralph, this is the field." Boy was he right. There was nothing around us for as far as you could see. I said, "The town is back there pointing to the lone water tower and little strip mall which was the only place to shop in Woodbury at the time." When Dr. Marks said, "This is the field," what he meant was this was the primary service area that I was to cover." He went on to say, "Ralph, you must imagine what God is preparing to do in this community over the next twenty-five years under your leadership." Who stays in one place for that many years I thought to myself. Andi and I prayed about our decision and felt God was leading us to Woodbury so we accepted.

***Raising the sign on our new church property at
1583 Radio Drive, Woodbury, MN***

After a four day training in Milwaukee, Wisconsin, I was on my own. My first task was to canvass the entire community and invite people without a church affiliation to consider becoming part of a new church. There were days I thought the entire world was Roman Catholic. Little by little I began to find people interested in being part of this new vision. After knocking on 3,800 doors, we secured the Woodbury High School cafeteria for a temporary worship site. On November 2nd, 1980, King of Kings Lutheran Church held its first service with 300 in attendance. Wow, you might say, what a great start! Yet I must be honest and say we had a few ringers in that number. Andrea's family came, the children's choir from Augustana and their families came just in case no one showed up. After counting the attendance sheets at the end of the day there were 100 prospective people from Woodbury.

One month later we started Sunday school with 26 children and 5 teachers, a modest beginning. As the word got around town more people and families began to come and express interest in becoming part of this new congregation. On October 18, 1981, King of Kings Lutheran Church became an official congregation of the Lutheran

Church in America with 262 baptized members. Synod President, Herbert Chilstrom, was there to celebrate and deliver the message. It was his 50th birthday so we hosted a cake and coffee time following the service in his honor.

Our first permanent church home, June 30, 1985

Many are called by God into ministry, but few are chosen to serve as mission developers. As an associate pastor I had responsibility for a few ministries, but now I had full responsibility for everything. Where I once had an office to go to each day, now my office was in the basement of our home, complete with mimeograph in our laundry room. From humble beginnings King of Kings grew rapidly. On June 30th, 1985 the congregation moved to its permanent home at 1583 Radio Drive. The building was 7,200 sq. feet about half the size of the high school space we were renting. With more than four hundred members we offered two worship services because we could only seat one hundred seventy-five comfortably.

The original color of the church was a crème paint on cedar siding. The paint did not last long and in two years we needed to repaint the exterior. The committee chose a smoke blue, often called Norwegian blue for the new color. To make a long story short, the blue paint was brighter than it was planned to be and our church became the talk of the town. Folks wondered what in heaven's name had we done to the church. There's a story that someone in city hall told questioning folks that Pastor Olsen was color blind and thought it was gray. King of Kings soon became known as the "Smurf Church," named for the little blue Smurfs in cartoons. God had a different plan for soon the color would become our calling card. New residents would call the church to ask where we were located and when told, King of Kings is the blue church on Radio Drive, they knew exactly where to find us.

As the church was growing and expanding so was our family. Andi and I are blessed with three beautiful daughters, Erica, Emily and Elise. Each delivery was memorable in its own way, but as I recall the drive to the hospital for Erica's birth stands out in my memory. It was winter, February 1st and we were coming across the Kellogg Street Bridge in St. Paul on our way to United Hospital. Having gone to pre-natal classes I wanted to be a good coach for my bride. As I was driving, I was trying to record the timing of the labor pains so I could tell the doctor. Suddenly we hit a patch of ice and we started to skid, calmly my wife said, "Put the pad down, concentrate on your driving and please get us there safely." We did. I parked the car in the emergency lot and made Andi walk in while I carried the bags. As soon as the nurses saw Andi they got a wheelchair and whisked her away, while I was left to fill out paperwork. When I got to the room the doctor was there and said it wouldn't be long. He was right. Suddenly there she was, Erica Lynne, a beautiful baby girl with red hair. I was so proud she had red hair, for by now my red hair had been replaced with a distinguished gray. On January 12, 1984 Emily was born and she had red hair, too. Emily was the smallest of our daughters at birth and somehow always seemed to be placed in the nursery by the larger babies. As people would pass by the nursery they would look at her through the window and say what a little peanut she was. Emily may have been small in stature, but she was mighty in Spirit. Our neighbor, Wally Perlt called her "peepers" because her eyes were always wide open. Elise was born on March 29, 1987, and this time, she did not have red hair. Elise was a beautiful brunette with darker skin tone than her sisters. Neighbor Wally had a special name for each girl: Erica America, Peepers and Cuz!

My beautiful family, Elise, Emily, Andrea, and Erica

Every parent is proud of their children, yet not all children have the label, PK's (preacher kids). It is not always easy to be the pastor's child because they are often in the public eye. Being PK's may not have always been easy for them, but they never seemed to complain, at least to their father. When Erica was in confirmation class I happened to be the teacher. Some of her friends would say, "Your dad's the pastor, so why don't you know the answer?" I recall she replied something like this, "Do you think we sit around our house every day reading the Bible and praying? We're just like any other family."

*Family Picture at Erica and Jeffrey's wedding
reception at Mendakota County Club*

Children grow up so fast. Suddenly, one day a young man comes to ask permission to marry your daughter. Jeffrey Reistad grew up on the East Side of St. Paul and they met on line. I can truly say Jeffrey is Erica's soul mate and part of God's plan for her life. I was thrilled to add another male to the family. When the wedding plans began I announced that I wanted to be a father of the bride on the day of the wedding and have someone else do the service. "What?' my daughters said in unison, 'you baptized us, confirmed us and now in the biggest moment of Erica's life you're just going to sit, that's not acceptable!" They won the day and I did give the wedding message.

It was July 8th, 2006 and I stood with my beautiful daughter waiting to walk her down the aisle. Everyone who knows me will tell you I am emotional. Many thought there was no way I would get down the aisle without crying! Well, I did it, not one tear. It seemed like I had barely sat down next to Andi and it was time for me to give the wedding message. I spoke on the theme of "Roots and Wings." As parents you are to raise your children grounded in faith and values and then give them wings to fly into their own life's journey. All went well until the very end of the homily when suddenly a "big crocodile tear" began to slowly slide down the right check of my face. Everyone could see it and expected that tear would be followed by a flood of tears. I quickly said, "Whoa, it's only one tear," and that was all because Andi and my hearts were filled with such joy and happiness. I look forward to the day when Emily and Elise find their soul mates because as I discovered that day it is a unique experience to be the father and the pastor of the bride.

How does one begin to summarize thirty years of ministry serving one congregation? I never imagined I would serve one congregation that long, but God kept presenting new opportunities for ministry to our rapidly growing congregation and community. A dear friend and man of great faith, Glen Holmquist, gave me a gift I would use as an illustration many times in those 30 years - a three-legged stool. The seat of the stool represented the people and the legs were the pillars upon which the congregation would stand – worship – learning - serving. In worship, we celebrate our communal relationship with God and fellowship with others. As followers of Jesus Christ we are to continue growing in faith through Bible study and prayer. In serving we reach out to others in and beyond our congregation with compassion and love. The legs were connected by a red heart, which symbolized Jesus Christ, for if Christ is not at the center of all you do, then the church is nothing more than a social club.

The pastoral ministry is unlike many other vocations because you develop deep relationships with the people you shepherd. You walk by their side in times of joy and sadness, success and failure. During my ministry at King of Kings I officiated at 1,020 baptisms, 287 weddings and 245 funerals. There are far too many events and stories for all of them to be included in this book so I have selected several that impacted my ministry.

Jennifer Lynne Olson baptism with her parents
Paul and Lynne Olson and me

Jennifer Lynne Olson was the first child baptized for our new congregation. When Erica was born Jennifer's parents brought her to the hospital and said, "Jennie this is your first friend, Erica." Jennie and Erica have been friends ever since. Of course, there is something special about baptizing your own children because you have the privilege to be their parent and pastor.

The first wedding in our new congregation was celebrated in the bride and groom's home because we did not have a building in 1982. It was a second marriage for the couple as both of their spouses had died of cancer. In fact, they met each other in the hospital during the long days they spent at the bed side of their loved one. The wedding was an intimate gathering of friends on a cold, snowy January night. What I remember about the wedding was the bride's love of candles, so we had a candlelight service in the family room with a soft fire glowing in It was a beautiful and intimate setting for a wedding and a reminder that a wedding doesn't have to be a large production. Jesus said, "Wherever two or three gather in my name I will be there in the midst of them. I had no doubt that God's Spirit filled the room that night.

Baptisms and weddings are celebrations of joy and new life. I remember when we decided to do baptisms once a month after the last service because there were so many being brought for baptism that to include baptisms in the service would mean longer services that would cause parking lot and entry space chaos. On August 14, 2005 I had the privilege to baptize the most children in one day – 14! I'm not sure, but that number is one that I believe will stand for many years.

Over the years some of the same guests came to the different weddings I officiated so I felt it was important to write a new, personal message for each couple because I didn't want people to say, "I've heard this message before, I think he just changed the names of the bride and groom."

On the other hand, funerals were difficult and very emotional for me. Looking back in my clergy records I discovered I had officiated at 25 funerals for persons under the age of 25 in the first 25 years of ministry at King of Kings, a most unusual fact. In January of 1984 four children were born in one week – Emily Olsen, Jacob Porter,

Jennifer Pallas and Michael Preller. I use to jokingly say this was our internal evangelism program to grow the church. My mentor, Gary Langness would say "It will be years before you receive any offering from them."

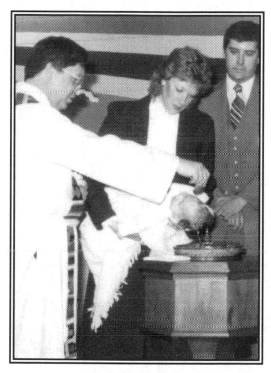

Michael Preller's baptism with his parents Marcia and Dave and me

Michael would spend much of his life in the hospital as the doctors tried to discover the cause of his condition. His parents spent long hours by his bedside. In the beginning I had difficulty visiting them in the hospital because I felt I was suppose to have answers for them. Wasn't I the trained theologian? What comfort and hope could I offer them? I remember Pastor Gary Langness saying we don't have the answers, but what we can do is humbly offer "the ministry of presence." We are chosen by the Holy Spirit to walk with them and show that we care so they do not feel alone in their journey. Michael's parents, Dave and Marcia, taught me so much during Michael's short life. Michael died at the tender age of 5 ½ years. Often in situations like this a couple will experience such extreme stress in their own relationship that their marriage will end in divorce. Dave and Marcia experienced many difficult days and long, lonely nights lovingly caring for Michael. They showed me each day what it truly means to love for better or worse, in sickness and in health for as long as one lives. A beautiful Colorado spruce tree is planted on the west side of the church building surrounded by a flower garden in Michael's memory. During Advent and Epiphany hundreds of small lights are lit on the tree as a reminder to all people that even in the darkness Christ's love shines forth as a beacon of hope for all.

Sometimes, it is a phone call in the night that awakens you or it can be a knock at your door. Our first friends in the neighborhood when we came to Woodbury were the Perlts: Wally, Dodie, Paul and Lisa. Little did I realize how close our families would become and the ministry events we would share in the years ahead. Paul, the oldest, received an appointment to the Coast Guard Academy after high school graduation. The academy wasn't always easy for Paul, but he graduated and was stationed in Florida. His mission was to fly over the Atlantic and Caribbean oceans searching for drug smugglers. One day there was a knock at my door. It was Wally with the news that Paul had died in a plane crash in Puerto Rico. This couldn't be true, but sadly it was. Paul was liked by everyone and his funeral was the largest in the history of the congregation. He was buried at Ft. Snelling National Cemetery with full military honors complete with a military plane fly over. Paul was 27 years old when he died. He was survived by his wife, Helen and daughter, Alexis. Tragically, Alexis died in her sleep at the age of 4.

My wedding stories would easily fill an entire book. Couples had some pretty interesting ideas for their wedding day and there were times I had to say no, we won't be doing that, like the time the couple wanted their dog to be the ring bearer It didn't make me very popular, but in the end almost all of the couples were married by me. Sometimes as a pastor you receive some very unique gifts, like the little shepherd boy statue. This particular couple had been a challenge to work with in marriage education. They were very young and had not given marriage much thought about what it meant to spend the rest of your lives together. We worked through many hurdles to get them to their wedding day. After the ceremony they presented me with a box containing a gift they had picked especially for me, when I opened the box there was a little shepherd boy statue carrying a sheep upon his shoulders. The entire statue was covered with gold fleck paint. What on earth would I do with this? Some pastor friends joked that we should join together and have a religious art garage sale some day with all the treasures we had received in our ministries. I decided the shepherd boy would go to the newest member on the church staff. Each new staff member had to prominently display the statue in their office until the next staff member came along and then they had the joy of passing it on. Ironically, there were staff members who really liked the statue and did not want to surrender it when their turn ended. Several hundred weddings, each unique in their own ways, certainly the most memorable was my daughter, Erica's wedding and the weddings of several nieces and nephew.

One memory I will always cherish was the first youth trip to Bethphage Mission in Axtell Nebraska. Where is Axtell, Nebraska you ask ? As best as I can explain, Bethphage is 12 miles directly south from Kearney which is located at the intersection of Interstate 80 and County Road 44. You know you are getting close to Axtell when you see the big yellow happy face on the town water tower. On that first trip we went with my friend, Pastor Bill Bohline, and the youth from his church. We arrived in the evening after a ten hour bus ride. We unpacked at the retreat center which was to be our home for the next seven days. The next morning was Sunday so after breakfast we walked to the chapel for church. The first people we met were slightly handicapped and welcomed us with open arms. Eldred was the head usher and he greeted us saying, "Hello, mah buddy." As more residents came the severity of their disabilities increased and I began to see looks of fear in our group's eyes. Worship was loud and had several nerve-wracking moments for our group.

1983 Youth Trip to Bethphage Mission Chapel Service

After chapel we went back to the retreat center to debrief and when we asked who wanted to go home it was almost unanimous that the group did not want to stay any longer. Bill and I told the group we were there for the week and the people needed our help. Each day we worked in different areas with the guests and each day our kids began to see beyond the disabilities and would come back with amazing stories of who they worked with and how much fun it was. When the next Saturday came and we were preparing to leave a number of the guests helped us take our things to the bus and told us they would miss us and please come back. Numerous moist eyes were seen as we drove away from Bethphage which told me hearts and lives had been changed by this experience. Our suburban young adults came to realize that all people are God's children and just want to be loved. In John 15:13 Jesus said, "Greater love has no man than this; that he lay down his life for his friends." Our group had given their lives to these special folks and and many more trips to Bethphage followed in the coming years. As younger youth heard the stories retold they were inspired to become a part of the Bethphage trip history.

In the beginning I wasn't sure why God was calling me to the ministry, yet throughout the years in moments of reflection I remembered sitting on that park bench in Brainerd, Minnesota where I believe God spoke to me in the wind saying, "Trust me and I will guide you." I did and God led me on an amazing journey, to people and places near and far.

First visit to Tumaini University, Irina, Tanzania with Drs. Mary and Arne Blomquist, Pastor Gary Langness, Emmanuel and Mama Machunga, Bishop Mdegella and another are bishop

In 2,000 Pastor Gary Langness invited me to join him on a trip to Tanzania, East Africa. This was the beginning of a life changing experience for members of my congregation, my family and me. Gary had two rules for anyone who travelled with him: 1) don't be an ugly American, remember you are a guest in their country and 2) don't get on the plane if you don't want to have your life changed forever. Boy, was he right! I would make 5 more trips to Tanzania over the next ten years with eighty pilgrims coming with me. My biggest thrill came in 2008 when Emily, Elise, and Andi came with me. The Tanzanian people had waited for eight years for Mama Andi to come and when they heard she was coming I knew it would be a trip she would never forget.

The first day as our group arrived at Kilolo Parish as Andi got off the bus the women immediately whisked her away and dressed her in a special outfit so everyone would be able to recognize her and welcome her. I thought to myself, it's fairly obvious to recognize my wife by the color of her skin and because she's always by my side. Now it was the male leaders who took me away to present me with a special shirt they had crafted . Without a doubt it was the nicest shirt I had ever received, but there was a problem. It was five sizes too small! Not to be deterred from their task, the men gathered around and somehow managed to get the shirt on me. As we went outside to join the celebration Andi said to me, "We'll have to cut that shirt off from you tonight because there is no way you'll be able to take it off yourself." I got the shirt off without using scissors!.

The Tanzanian people are gracious and faith-filled. For them the sun comes up and the sun goes down and that's a day. It's funny because they all wear watches, but they live on Tanzanian time, which means one never knows what time they may arrive for events. As Pastor Langness said, "Go with the flow and be gracious."

*My family and our dear friends Pastors Pascal
and Dorcas Azzaza and their children*

I have always enjoyed singing and one memory I carried in my heart every day was the beauty and pure acappella sound of their singing. I remember asking a young woman, Blandina Sawike, who directed the choir if they ever got tired of singing. "Oh no, pastor, when you know the one to whom you sing, your joy never ceases," Their faith is simple and pure.

The essence of life for these wonderful people is grounded in two core values, first, a relationship to God and second, a relationship to neighbor. I called this the "Be and Do Principle."

Pastor Gabriel Makongwa told me that Americans are all about DO. Our lives are filled with never ending schedules, goals, wants and to-do lists. We rush and hurry from project to project, place to place. One day we realize we have so much, but our life seems empty. We struggle for meaning and purpose. We don't know who we are which is BE. He said, "When you know whose you are then you will know what you are to do." We forget what we have is not ours, but rather a blessing from God to be used and shared with others.

Students of St. Margaret's Academy at lunch

I experienced a gracious and faith-filled people whose genuineness touched my soul. I treasure the times and experiences I shared with Drs. Arne and Mary Blomquist, Pastor Richard Lubawa and so many others for your incredible ministry at Tumaini University – Iringa. Thank you Pastor Benjamin, Anna and the Ngede family for your gracious hospitality. The Ngede's hosted almost every group that came to Iringa. The Ngede family was the first Tanzanian family to come to the United States as part of the "Bega Kwa Bega" companion program with the St. Paul Area Synod of the Evangelical Lutheran Church in America. "Bega Kwa Bega in Swahili means working together, shoulder to shoulder, hand in hand.

An evening at the Ngede's was always a special treat. Anna would serve her famous "Forest Lake buns," that she learned to make while they were in America. Thank you Ngede family for the food, the fellowship and the singing after dinner that made the night pass so quickly.

Thank you, Dr. Mark and Linda Jacobson for dedicating your lives to improving health care and the quality of life for the people of Tanzania at Selian Lutheran Hospital and the Arusha Lutheran Medical Center. You are more than a missionary sponsored family to my family. You are our family and we are blessed to know you.

Thank you Mama Margaret Tesha, you came to my office in Minnesota with a hope and a prayer to build a school in Tanzania. I knew after that first meeting we were going to do just that. Your vision and desire to give children an education inspired me and my congregation to help. Today hundreds of children have a bright future because you had a God inspired vision.

Offering prayers of thanksgiving for the past and hope for the future, because our future rests with our children

My daughters, Emily and Elise, are teachers. Emily is an English Language Learner teacher at New Visions Academy, a charter school in NE Minneapolis, MN. Elise is a K-2nd grade science teacher at Cherokee Heights Elementary in St. Paul, MN. Both girls teach in multi-ethnic schools where discipline and issues other than teaching take up a good portion of their day. It was quite another experience for Emily when she stayed on for another month in Tanzania in 2008 to teach at St. Margaret's Academy in Tanzania. Students are excited and proud to be in school. Teachers are respected for their knowledge and passion to see students excel. Education for a Tanzanian child is a great blessing that not all children get the opportunity to study. Primary education cost is covered by the government.

The fact is secondary education costs roughly 300,000 Tsh ($300 US) which is the average annual income of a Tanzanian family. Besides the cost, the student must pass the national examination to qualify for admission. If they qualify they need to find a sponsor to pay the tuition. This means that not every child who qualifies academically gets to go on in their studies. There is great celebration for a family if their child is blessed to move forward and heart break for those who cannot. At St. Margaret's Academy they sing a song about education. "Education is the key to life. No working without an education. When I grow up, I want to be a doctor. Can I be a doctor without education? No, no you can't be a doctor without education, education, education." The song can have many verses as the children sing about their dreams all of which need an education.

Our family was blessed to provide scholarship support for Lightness Magaya and David Azzaza which was not only a blessing to them and their families, but to our family knowing our gifts were shaping and changing the future of two wonderful young people.

The end of my ministry at my congregation after thirty years of service did not end as I hoped. Through a series of difficult events I left my position. It is not easy to leave something you loved and to which you dedicated your life's work. As I reflect upon those years I can only celebrate the wonders and miracles that God inspired and blessed through our shared ministry.

Not every pastor gets the privilege to be a mission developer. Not every pastor will have so many opportunities to serve God's people locally and around the world. I was blessed to do both. I cherish the memories and the people I came to know. What was accomplished with God's help and the faithfulness of his people is my legacy in ministry. Nothing can take that away.

It's been said when a door closes God opens a window to a new life and new opportunities. After a twenty-two month journey with God I received a new ministry and opportunity to serve him. I joined the staff of the Union Gospel Mission in St. Paul as the Planned Giving Officer. The Mission seeks to help the homeless, the hungry, the addicted, single women, moms and their children, chemically addicted and those released from prison or jail. For 110 years the Mission has shared the love of Christ with open arms to anyone who desires to begin a new life. My many years in ministry have surely paved the way for this new opportunity.

From humble beginnings and with the grace and blessing of God I sought to "walk the talk" with compassion and integrity, believing in God's guidance and living my life as a testament to my personal mission statement: to be a reflection of Christ's love every day through my words and actions that I might be a messenger of hope and encouragement to the people God places in my path.

My life and ministry have been inspired by the following story and I include it for you to consider in your life's journey. A man discovered hundreds of star fish washed up on the shore. Knowing they would die if not returned to the sea, he bent down and began to gently throwing them back into the water one star fish at a time. A passerby saw what the man was doing, stopped and said, "What are you doing?

Do you think you can save them all?" Without saying a word the man picked up another star fish and as he gently threw it into the water he said, "Well, it made a difference to that one."

Matthew 6: 14–16 says, "You are the light of the world. A city on a hill cannot be hidden. Nor does one light a lamp and put it under a basket, but on a table so that it gives light to all those in the house. Let your light so shine before others that they may see your good works and give glory to your father in heaven." Each of us is given the opportunity to be a light of hope and love to the people God places in your path each day.

Mother Teresa, a Roman Catholic nun, let her personal light shine over the poorest of the poor in India. She said every time she looked into the face of the sick and dying she saw the face of Jesus. I have been inspired by a quote from her. "I am not sure exactly what heaven will be like, but I know that when we die and it comes time for God to judge us, he will not ask, "How many good things have you done in your life?" rather he will ask, "How much love did you put into what you did?"

I always knew I could not change the world alone, but I could cast a stone across the water creating a ripple effect that would slowly spread to others. May my story inspire you to be bold, be courageous and be committed to making a difference each day, one moment and one person at a time.

Soli Deo Gloria!

My grandson, Samuel James, off to explore his world and his future

Printed in the United States
By Bookmasters